Classifying Living Things

Insects

Andrew Solway

Chicago, Illinois

www.heinemannraintree.com
Visit our website to find out more information about Heinemann-Raintree books.

To order:
☎ Phone 888-454-2279
▣ Visit www.heinemannraintree.com to browse our catalog and order online.

Edited by Catherine Clarke and Claire Throp
Designed by Victoria Bevan and AMR Design, Ltd.
Original illustrations © Capstone Global Library, LLC.
Illustrations by David Woodroffe
Picture research by Hannah Taylor

Printed and bound in China by Leo Paper Group

13 12 11 10 09
10 9 8 7 6 5 4 3 2 1

Library of Congress Cataloging-in-Publication Data

Solway, Andrew.
    Classifying insects / Andrew Solway.
      p. cm. -- (Classifying living things)
Summary: Explains what insects are and how they differ from others animals, with an overview of the life cycle of a variety of insects, including ants, bees, cockroaches, grasshoppers, dragonflies, and butterflies.
Includes bibliographical references (p.   ) and index.
    ISBN 978-1-4329-2355-6 (lib. bdg. : hardcover) -- ISBN 978-1-4329-2365-5 (pbk.)
    1. Insects--Classification--Juvenile literature. 2. Insects--Juvenile literature. [1. Insects.] I. Title. II Series.
    QL468 .S66 2003
    595.7--dc21
                                    2002015403

Acknowledgments

For Harriet, Eliza and Nicholas.

We would like to thank the following for allowing their pictures to be reproduced in this publication: Digital Vision p. 23; FLPA p. 7 (Minden Pictures/Piotr Naskrecki); naturepl pp. 10 (Mike Wilkes), 22 (Dietmar Nill); Photolibrary pp. 4 (OSF/TC Nature), 5 (OSF/Alastair Shay), 11, 14, 26, 27 (OSF), 15 (OSF/Chris Perrins), 16 (OSF/Mantis Wildlife Films), 18 (Keith Ringland), 21 (OSF/Brian Kennedy), 25 (Ott Ott), 28 (Marco Simoni), 29 (Geoff Du Feu); Science Photo Library p. 13 (Gregory Dimijian); Warren Photographic pp. 17, 19, 20, 24 (Kim Taylor).

Cover photograph of a dragonfly and a caterpillar, reproduced with permission of Photolibrary/ imagebroker.net/Ingo Schulz.

We would like to thank Ann Fullick for her invaluable assistance in the preparation of this book, and Catherine Armstrong for her help with the first edition.

Contents

Some words are shown in bold, **like this**. You can find out what they mean by looking in the glossary.

The natural world is full of an incredible variety of **organisms**. They range from tiny bacteria, too small to see, to giant redwood trees over 100 meters (330 feet) tall. With such a bewildering variety of life, it is hard to make sense of the living world. For this reason, scientists classify living things by sorting them into groups.

Classifying the living world

Sorting organisms into groups makes them easier to understand. Scientists try to classify living things in a way that tells you how closely one group is related to another. They look at everything about an organism, from its color and shape to the **genes** inside its **cells**. They even look at **fossils** to give them clues about how living things have changed over time. Then the scientists use all this information to sort the millions of different things into groups.

Scientists do not always agree about the group an organism belongs to, so they collect as much evidence as possible to find its closest relatives.

You can find insects in every corner of the world. Tiny insects like this ice bug live on ice and snowfields high in the mountains. Insects like this have special "antifreeze" in their bodies to stop them from freezing in the cold.

From kingdoms to species

Classification allows us to measure the **biodiversity** of the world. To begin the classification process, scientists divide living things into huge groups called **kingdoms**. For example, plants are in one kingdom, while animals are in another. There is some argument among scientists about how many kingdoms there are—at the moment most agree that there are five! Each kingdom is then divided into smaller groups called **phyla** (singular *phylum*), and the phyla are further divided into **classes**. The next subdivision is into **orders**. Within an order, organisms are grouped into **families** and then into a **genus** (plural *genera*), which contains a number of closely related **species**. A species is a single kind of organism, such as a mouse or a buttercup. Members of a species can reproduce and produce fertile offspring together.

Scientific names

Many living things have a common name, but these can cause confusion when the same organism has different names around the world. To avoid problems, scientists give every species a two-part Latin name, which is the same all over the world. The first part of the scientific name tells you the genus the organism belongs to. The second part tells you the exact species. The desert locust, for example, has the scientific name *Schistocerca gregaria*, while the American grasshopper is *Schistocerca americana*.

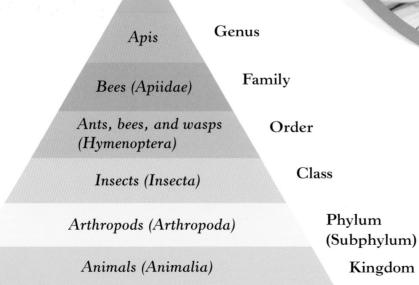

mellifera	Species
Apis	Genus
Bees (Apiidae)	Family
Ants, bees, and wasps (Hymenoptera)	Order
Insects (Insecta)	Class
Arthropods (Arthropoda)	Phylum (Subphylum)
Animals (Animalia)	Kingdom

This diagram shows the full classification for a honeybee (*Apis mellifera*).

Insects are part of a **phylum** of animals called **arthropods**. Arthropods do not have bones: instead they have a tough outer "skin" called an exoskeleton. They move around on jointed legs. Crabs and shrimps (crustaceans), spiders and scorpions (arachnids), and insects are the most important arthropod groups.

Scientists think that the ancestors (relatives in the past) of the arthropods were a group of worms called the annelids (earthworms are modern annelid worms). Like annelid worms, arthropods are divided into sections, or **segments**.

Body armor

An arthropod's exoskeleton is like a suit of armor. It is made up of hard, protective plates connected by flexible joints, which allow the animal to move. The exoskeleton supports the arthropod's body and protects its soft insides.

The exoskeleton is a fixed size—it cannot grow with the rest of the animal. This means that every so often an arthropod has to shed its exoskeleton, which is known as **molting**. A new exoskeleton forms underneath, so when the old one splits, the animal is ready to climb out of it. For a short time the new exoskeleton is soft. While it is soft the arthropod swells up, to give itself growing room.

Six-legged flyers

Insects are different from other arthropods in several important ways, which allow us to classify them clearly:
- Almost all insects live on land.
- The insect body is divided into three segments—head, thorax (the middle part), and **abdomen** (the back part).

Insect power

Insects are the most successful group of living things on Earth. Nearly three-fourths of all **species** are insects. There are about 200 million times more insects than there are people!

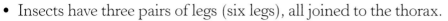

- Insects have three pairs of legs (six legs), all joined to the thorax.
- Many insects have wings—they are the only flying arthropods—so they can reach many different habitats.
- Insects have a layer of waterproof wax over their cuticle (tough outer layer), and their eggs have a waterproof coating, too.
- They have **compound eyes**, which are very sensitive to movement.

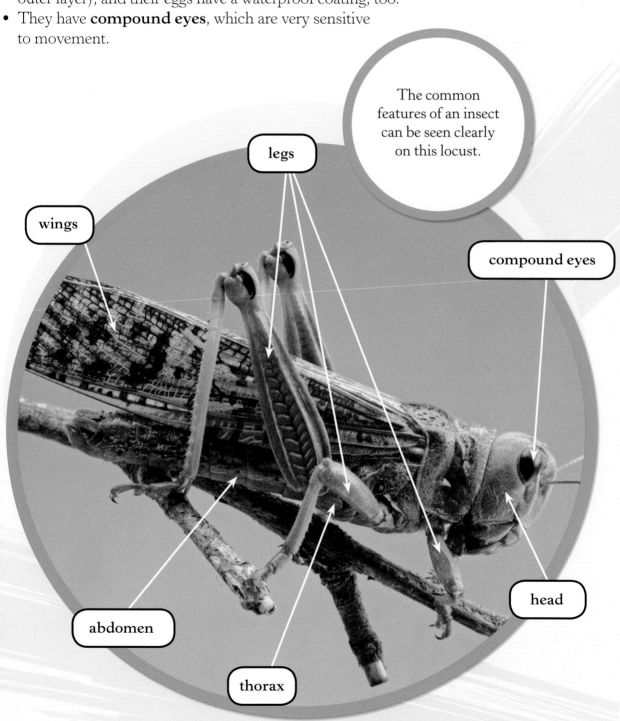

The common features of an insect can be seen clearly on this locust.

legs

wings

compound eyes

abdomen

head

thorax

There are 28 different **orders** of insects. Some, such as cockroaches, have changed very little since the first insects appeared about 300 million years ago. Other orders, such as flies, appeared later.

This table shows a selection of insect orders.

Type	Order	No. of species	Example
Wingless insects	Bristletails (Archeaognatha)	250	bristletail
	Silverfish (Thysanura)	330	silverfish
Insects with incomplete metamorphosis	Mayflies (Ephemeroptera)	about 2,000	March brown mayfly
	Dragonflies (Odonata)	about 5,000	green clearwing dragonfly
	Cockroaches (Blattodea)	about 3,500	American cockroach
	Termites (Isoptera)	about 2,200	drywood termite
	Mantids (Mantodea)	about 1,800	praying mantis
	Earwigs (Dermaptera)	about 1,200	earwig
	Grasshoppers and crickets (Orthoptera)	over 20,000	desert locust
	Stick and leaf insects (Phasmatoidea)	about 2,700	pink-winged stick insect
	Parasitic lice (Phthiraptera)	over 3,000	human louse
	Bugs (Hemiptera)	about 67,500	bedbug
Insects with complete metamorphosis	Lacewings (Neuroptera)	about 5,500	lacewing
	Beetles (Coleoptera)	about 300,000	stag beetle
	Scorpion flies (Mecoptera)	about 475	scorpion fly
	Fleas (Siphonaptera)	over 2,200	oriental rat flea
	Two-winged flies (Diptera)	about 90,000	Crane fly
	Caddis flies (Trichoptera)	about 10,000	caddis fly
	Butterflies and moths (Lepidoptera)	about 150,000	peacock butterfly
	Ants, wasps, and bees (Hymenoptera)	about 280,000	leaf cutter ant

Life cycles

Nearly all insects hatch from eggs. But the way an insect develops varies according to its type. The changes an insect goes through during its life cycle are called **metamorphosis**. In insect orders, such as dragonflies and grasshoppers, the young look similar to adults when they hatch from the egg. At this stage they are known as **nymphs**. As the nymphs grow and **molt**, they gradually develop wings and become more like adults. This kind of life cycle is called **incomplete metamorphosis**.

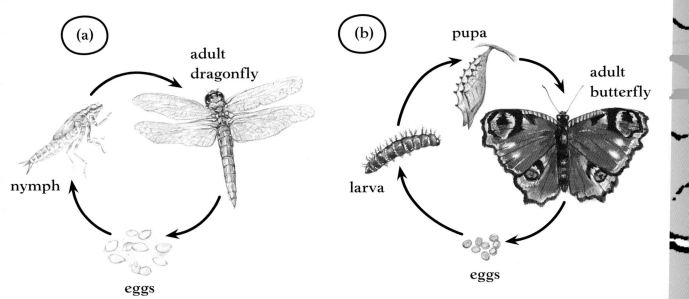

(a) adult dragonfly — nymph — eggs

(b) pupa — adult butterfly — larva — eggs

The young of insects such as butterflies, flies, and bees are very different from the adults. They are called **larvae** (one of them is called a larva). A larva is an eating machine. As it eats, it grows and molts several times. But it does not change to become more like an adult—it just gets bigger. When the larva reaches its full size, it molts one more time and becomes a **pupa** (chrysalis).

The pupa does not feed or move. The outside is a hard, protective case. Inside, an incredible transformation takes place. The larva turns itself into an adult insect. This kind of insect life cycle is called **complete metamorphosis**.

Metamorphosis means "change." Dragonflies change gradually as they grow from eggs into adults. This is called incomplete metamorphosis (a). Butterflies, on the other hand, change in a series of jumps, from an egg to a larva (a caterpillar) to a pupa to an adult. This is called complete metamorphosis (b).

Insect wings

The very first insects had no wings. A few close relatives of these earliest insects are still found today. There are also some insect **species** that once had wings, but no longer have them. This happened because they live in places where wings are of no use—for example, in tree trunks or underground.

Many insects have two pairs of wings. But in some insect groups one pair has become **adapted** for some other purpose. In beetles, for instance, the front pair of wings has become a pair of hard, protective wing cases.

There are more types of beetle than of any other **organism**. They are the largest **order** of insects. Ladybugs, weevils, fireflies, and woodworms are all types of beetle.

What is a beetle?

In all beetles, only the hind wings are used for flying. The front wings are hard, armored wing cases that cover the beetle's back. The hind wings fold away under these wing cases.

The type of mouthparts (jaws) an insect has depends on what it eats. Most beetles have biting mouthparts, but some **species** feed in different ways (for instance, sucking up their food). Their mouthparts have **adapted** to suit these ways of feeding. All beetles undergo **complete metamorphosis**.

African dung beetle—a smelly feast!

- 7,000 species of dung beetles
- Rolls dung into balls to make them easier to move
- Helps break down animal wastes
- Beetles work as a team to manage large dung balls

Beetle feeding

Beetles live and feed in a huge variety of places. Some, such as ladybugs and tiger beetles, are **predators**. Ladybugs are popular with farmers and gardeners because they eat insects such as aphids, which can damage flowers and crops. Other beetles feed on plants. Leaf beetles eat leaves, while woodworms and deathwatch beetles eat wood. Weevils are plant pests. Many of them eat important farm crops.

Many species of beetle are scavengers. Some eat dead leaves and rotting vegetation, while dung beetles eat animal dung. This might not sound very appealing, but these beetles play an important part in turning animal wastes into rich, fertile soil.

Stag beetle—horned fighter
- Adult beetles feed on sap and honeydew
- Male beetles have enlarged jaws that look like horns
- "Horns" may be brightly colored
- Males fight over females for a chance to mate

Finding a mate

Adult beetles need to find another beetle of the opposite sex in order to **mate** and produce offspring. Different species do this in different ways. Female chafers and click beetles produce a special scent that attracts males. Male fireflies produce light, which they use to signal to females at night. Most female fireflies cannot fly. They glow in response to the male's light, and then males drop down to mate.

Ants, Bees, and Wasps

The main thing that separates ants, bees, and wasps from other insects is their "wasp waist." Part of the **abdomen** is very thin and flexible. Some ants, bees, and wasps are social insects—they live in large colonies (groups). But there are also many **species** that live alone.

Parasitic wasps

Many wasp species are **parasitic**. Their **larvae** feed on or inside other plants and animals, eventually killing their **host**. They then become **pupae** and hatch out as adults.

Parasitic wasps lay their eggs on or in all kinds of plants and animals. Many species lay their eggs in the caterpillars of various insects.

Solitary wasps and bees

Many species of wasp and bee are solitary—they live alone, only meeting with other wasps to **mate**. Solitary bees and wasps dig small nests for their eggs and put in enough food to feed the larvae from birth until they become adults.

Wasps, figs, and extinction?

Fig trees are very a important food source for many different species of animals. Each type of fig tree is **pollinated** by a different species of fig wasp. Some of these wasps live their whole life within a single flower and fruit! However, if anything threatens the survival of either fig trees or wasps, both become endangered, because they cannot survive without each other.

In bees and nonparasitic wasps, the long egg tube has become a stinger. Solitary wasps use this to kill **prey**. Solitary bees collect **pollen** and **nectar** to feed their larvae. They make honey from the nectar and fill the nest with honey and pollen.

Not all ants are **predators**. Leaf-cutter ants grow their own food. They cut small pieces from leaves and carry them to their nests. There they grow a fungus on the leaves. This fungus is their main food.

Bee sociable!

Ants, and some wasp and bee species, are social insects. They live in large nests, with a queen that lays all the eggs and many female workers that find food and care for the larvae. There are also a few males, whose job is to mate with new queens. In some ant species, large soldier ants guard the colony.

Ants dig their nests into the ground or pile up soil and other material in an anthill, while bees and wasps build nests in holes or on trees. Bee and wasp nests contain "combs" made up of many six-sided wax cells. These act as nurseries for the larvae and stores the honey.

13

You can find cockroaches almost anywhere. They live in deserts and swamps, on mountains and in cold areas, in burrows underground, in trees, and in caves. Some **species** live alongside humans in cities and towns.

Cockroaches

Cockroaches have a flattened body and long antennae. In all species a hard plate protects the head and the front of the body. Cockroaches are often found in places where humans live. Their flattened bodies fit into all kinds of cracks, where they hide during the day. At night they come out and scavenge for food.

Do you know ... how cockroaches survive?

Cockroaches have hardly changed over thousands of years and can survive almost anywhere. When they are in danger or stressed, they produce a special chemical that sends their body into a state where all the reactions of life slow down. They can remain hidden like this for weeks and even months, before emerging ready to find food and continue with normal life!

A cockroach's digestive system contains millions of tiny creatures called protozoa, which help it to digest its food. It can eat even tough materials like wood.

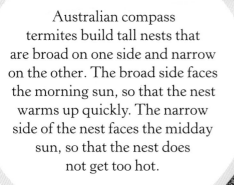

Australian compass termites build tall nests that are broad on one side and narrow on the other. The broad side faces the morning sun, so that the nest warms up quickly. The narrow side of the nest faces the midday sun, so that the nest does not get too hot.

Termites

Termites are closely related to cockroaches. Termites look kind of like large-headed ants. Most feed on dead and rotten wood. Like cockroaches, termites have tiny creatures called protozoa living in their **digestive systems**, which help them to **digest** tough food like wood.

A termite colony is started by a termite "king" and "queen." Millions of termites live there. Once the first termites are grown, they take over raising the young, leaving the queen to concentrate on laying eggs. She produces over 30,000 eggs a day.

There are several kinds of termite in a colony. Most are workers, which feed the **larvae**, find food, and build the nest. Soldiers defend the nest from enemies. Some soldiers have huge jaws, while others have a snout that produces a horrible chemical spray. Winged termites fly off to set up new colonies elsewhere.

Some African species build huge mounds over 7 meters (25 feet) tall. The mounds are chimneys that draw hot, stale air out of the nest. The nest itself contains galleries full of termite larvae, as well as food stores where the termites grow a kind of fungus found only in these nests.

Butterflies and moths belong to the same **order** as each other. They are the only insects that have thousands of tiny scales covering the surface of their wings. Often these scales form beautiful patterns and colors.

Patterned wings

In some **species**, the bright patterns on the wings of butterflies and moths are a warning that they are poisonous. Bright colors also help butterflies recognize their **mates**.

A butterfly or moth that is not poisonous cannot be brightly colored, because it will become easy food for a **predator**. So, some species have secret markings that are visible only to animals that can see ultraviolet light. Butterflies can see this type of light, but their enemies cannot.

Although they are small, butterflies can fly very long distances. Monarch butterflies, like these, migrate more than 8,000 kilometers (5,000 miles) every year, from Canada to northern Mexico.

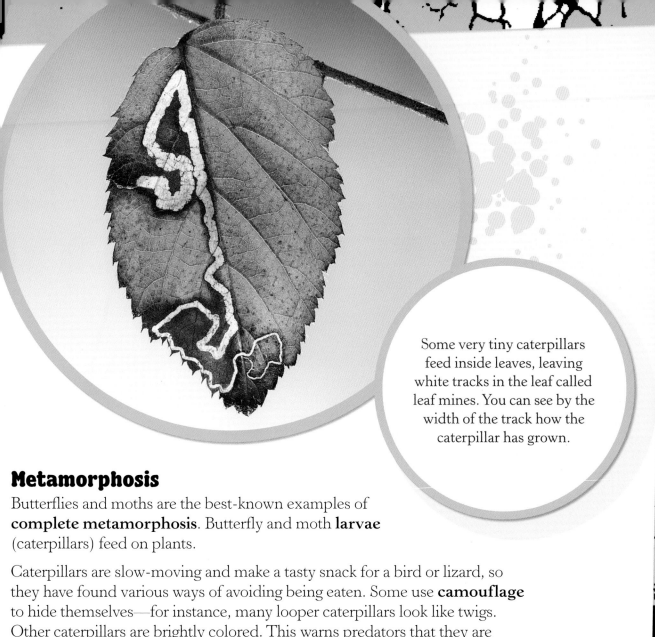

Some very tiny caterpillars feed inside leaves, leaving white tracks in the leaf called leaf mines. You can see by the width of the track how the caterpillar has grown.

Metamorphosis

Butterflies and moths are the best-known examples of **complete metamorphosis**. Butterfly and moth **larvae** (caterpillars) feed on plants.

Caterpillars are slow-moving and make a tasty snack for a bird or lizard, so they have found various ways of avoiding being eaten. Some use **camouflage** to hide themselves—for instance, many looper caterpillars look like twigs. Other caterpillars are brightly colored. This warns predators that they are poisonous to eat or are covered in itchy hairs or spikes.

Once a caterpillar is fully grown it becomes a **pupa** (chrysalis). Pupae have a hard outer case or a silk **cocoon** that protects the changing insect inside. When the adult emerges from the pupa, it is no longer a wormlike caterpillar, but rather a winged butterfly or moth.

Feeding

Like bees, butterflies and moths are flower specialists. The long tongues of butterflies and moths let them reach **nectar** in flowers that are too deep for other insects. Nectar is almost pure sugar. Since animals also need protein in their food, to repair and renew themselves, most adult butterflies and moths can live only for a few weeks. But a few live longer because they feed on protein-containing **pollen** as well as nectar. The zebra longwing butterfly, for instance, lives for up to six months.

Two-winged flies have only one pair of wings. But they are not poor fliers—they can fly backward, hover, turn on the spot, and even land upside down. The secret to their flying skill is a pair of structures just behind the wings, which look like balls on sticks. These are called halteres and are the remains of the fly's hind wings. They help the fly to balance in flight. Only two-winged flies have halteres.

Fly larvae

Female flies choose a place to lay their eggs that will help their **larvae** find the right food when they hatch. If the larvae eat plant-eating insects, for instance, the female lays her eggs on plants where these insects might be found. Other fly larvae are **parasites**. Botfly larvae, for instance, live just under the skin of large animals such as sheep. The female fly lays her eggs on the animal's skin, and the larvae burrow under the skin when they hatch.

Fly foods

A fly's mouthpart forms a tube that it uses to suck up liquid food. In some cases the food is already liquid, but the fly can also pump saliva (spit) onto the food, which turns the solid food into liquid.

Many kinds of fly are scavengers. As with beetles, these scavenger flies are important for breaking down dead animals and plants, producing richer soils.

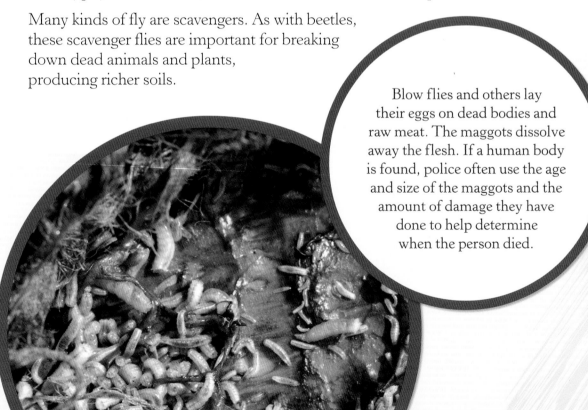

Blow flies and others lay their eggs on dead bodies and raw meat. The maggots dissolve away the flesh. If a human body is found, police often use the age and size of the maggots and the amount of damage they have done to help determine when the person died.

In this picture of a crane fly, you can see the fly's halteres. Most flies have good eyesight. Their huge **compound eyes** do not give as clear a view of the world as our eyes, but they are better at spotting movement.

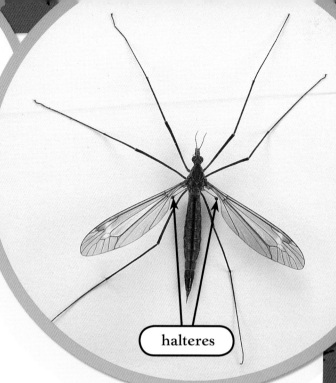

halteres

Some flies get their food from dung. Male dung flies gather around a fresh pile of dung, looking for females. When a female arrives, she **mates** with one of the males. Then she lays her eggs in the dung.

Other groups of flies, such as midges, mosquitoes, and horseflies, are bloodsuckers. They feed on the blood of large animals. But it is only the females who drink blood. They need protein from the blood to make their eggs. Males of these **species** feed on **nectar** from flowers.

Many other flies get at least part of their food from flowers. Hoverflies feed only on nectar. Their yellow and black stripes make them look like bees or wasps, but they are harmless.

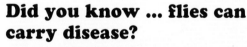

Did you know ... flies can carry disease?

Flies carry **microorganisms** from feces (bodily waste) and rotting meat onto other food, which can cause disease. In hot countries, mosquitoes carry tiny protozoa in their blood that cause the disease malaria. In a similar way, tsetse flies carry a disease called sleeping sickness. If an infected mosquito or tsetse fly feeds on a human, it may pass on the disease.

People often call any small insect a "bug." But in scientific terms, bugs are a large, varied **order** of insects with mouthparts that form a stiff, thin "beak." They use this beak for piercing and sucking up food. Most bugs feed on plant sap (fluid).

Bugs are split into two groups, based on the differences in their mouthparts. True bugs include brightly colored shield bugs and water bugs such as pond skaters. The other group includes aphids, cicadas, and treehoppers.

True bugs

In true bugs, part of the front wing is hardened, but the rest is clear and flexible. No other insects have this kind of wing. They can swing their beak forward to feed, which means they can feed on other things besides plant juices. A few bugs, such as pond skaters and assassin bugs, are **predators** that feed on other insects.

Shield bug—smelly herbivores

- Typical "shield-shaped" wing cases, often colorful and patterned
- Eats plants
- Stink glands on the **abdomen**
- Known as "stink bugs" because of the smell they leave on plants and on anyone who picks them up to take a look!

Some treehoppers have strangely shaped bodies. Some **species** look like thorns when they rest on plants.

Hoppers, cicadas, and aphids

Unlike true bugs, hoppers, cicadas, and aphids can only move their beak to the vertical position. All of them feed on plants, piercing through the outer surface to the juicy sap beneath.

The best-known hoppers are froghoppers and spittlebugs. The **nymphs** of these bugs produce a frothy white substance known as "cuckoo spit." This protects the nymphs from drying out and from being attacked by predators.

Cicada nymphs live underground, feeding on the sap of roots. Some live underground for 17 or 18 years. Adult cicadas live above ground, but only for a few weeks. Male cicadas produce a high buzzing or hissing "song" to attract females.

Aphids are tiny insects that feed on plants in large colonies (groups). Some aphids are pests on farms and in gardens, because they damage or sometimes kill the plants they feed on. Their numbers can grow incredibly fast. When food is plentiful, all aphid young are born female, and they do not need to **mate** to produce eggs. Each aphid can produce three to six young per day. The young grow very fast, becoming adults within a week.

Grasshoppers and crickets are medium-to-large insects with strong back legs that are good for jumping. All grasshoppers and crickets make sounds, and they also have "ears" to hear sounds. Their front wings are hardened to protect the large hind wings, which fold up like a fan.

Grasshoppers and crickets eat plants, but many will also eat animals. A few **species**, such as the mole cricket, are mainly **predators**.

Grasshopper lifestyles

Some grasshoppers and crickets live in the open, while others live mainly underground, or in caves. Grasshoppers and crickets that live in the open have long bodies. They protect themselves from predators in various ways. Some species are **camouflaged**. They may be colored in such a way that they are almost invisible when still, or they may look like twigs or leaves. Others are poisonous or produce foul-smelling liquid when attacked. These species often have bright warning colors.

Grasshoppers and crickets that live underground have shorter bodies and powerful front legs that they use for digging. Some species feed on the roots of plants, while others eat microscopic creatures in the soil.

Oedipoda caerulescens—the blue-winged grasshopper
- Plant-eater
- Long antennae
- Long back legs
- Blue, sail-like wings

Locust swarms

Most grasshoppers and crickets live alone. But some other species that live in hot lands change their behavior when there is plenty of food. They gather in huge swarms of billions of insects. These insects are called locusts.

Singing and dancing

Like cicadas, male grasshoppers and crickets sing to attract a **mate**. They make sounds either by rubbing part of the back leg against the hard front wing or by rubbing the front wings together. The sounds that they make can be loud, but the mole cricket has a way to make its song even louder. It digs a specially shaped burrow that amplifies the sounds so that they can be heard up to 2 kilometers (1.2 miles) away.

Do you know ... how mantises attack?

Mantises are close relatives of grasshoppers and crickets (they are also related to cockroaches). They are large insects with a triangular-shaped head. Mantises are predators, and they are masters of the surprise attack. Many species look like leaves, twigs, or flowers. They hold themselves absolutely still, with their large front legs held up. When a suitable victim comes near, the mantis shoots out its front legs and grabs it. The legs are covered in hooks and spines to help hold the **prey**.

Dragonflies and mayflies are two of the oldest **orders** of insects. They first appeared flying over ponds and swamps about 300 million years ago—that is about 70 million years before the first dinosaurs!

Both mayflies and dragonflies have long, slender bodies and two pairs of wings that cannot be folded away. The young **nymphs** of both groups live underwater and breathe through gills like fish.

Mayflies

Mayflies are medium-sized, summer insects. They have large front wings and smaller hind wings.

Mayfly nymphs live in streams and ponds, either swimming freely or burrowing into the stream or pond bed. The nymphs live underwater for up to three years. They filter food from the water or find it in the mud.

Just before the nymph is fully grown, it crawls out of the water. It then **molts** and becomes a dull-colored adult called a dun. This is not the true adult. It flies only a short way before it molts one more time and then becomes a true adult.

Male mayflies gather in swarms above the water. Females are attracted to these swarms, and they **mate** with the males. They then lay their eggs in the water.

Adult mayflies live a few days—just long enough to breed and lay eggs. They do not eat at all. Their **digestive system** is filled with air, which helps them fly better.

Dragonflies

Dragonflies are bigger than mayflies and often brightly colored. They have large eyes and short antennae. Like mayflies, they are often found near water. Both as nymphs and as adults, dragonflies are fierce **predators**.

Dragonfly nymphs live in water habitats. They have powerful jaws, which they can shoot out to grab **prey**. They live underwater for up to six years, before coming out of the water and molting.

The new dragonfly adults spend a few days or weeks hunting away from the water before returning to mate. When they are fully mature, males are often brilliantly colored. The males of some **species** help with the egg-laying, holding onto the female as she lays her eggs on or near the water.

Dragonfly—beautiful hunter

- Two pairs of wings that cannot be folded away
- Large **compound eyes** give excellent sight
- Hunts in the air
- Grabs prey with spiny legs

Did you know ... about giant dragonflies?

In the past, dragonflies were even bigger than they are today. Around 300 million years ago, some dragonflies had a wingspan of 75 centimeters (30 inches) — bigger than a duck's wings!

25

Have you ever had head lice? Children sometimes get them at school. They make your head itch and can sometimes be hard to get rid of. You are less likely to have had fleas, but you may have a pet dog or cat that has had them. Lice and fleas are not related, but all **species** in both **orders** are **parasites**. They ride around on mammals or birds, feeding on their blood or skin.

Lice

Lice are highly **adapted** to their parasitic life. They are tiny, wingless, dull-colored insects with a flattened body and short legs. They have strong claws, which they use to hang onto their **host**, and either piercing or chewing mouthparts. Some lice feed on small pieces of skin, but many species suck blood.

Lice live their whole lives on their host. Most simply hang onto fur or feathers, but curlew lice live in the hollow stems of the bird's wing feathers. Pelican lice live in the pelican's throat pouch. Female lice fasten their eggs to the host animal's fur or feathers using a hard, quick-drying "glue." The young lice that hatch from the eggs look similar to the adults. They **molt** three times before they are fully grown.

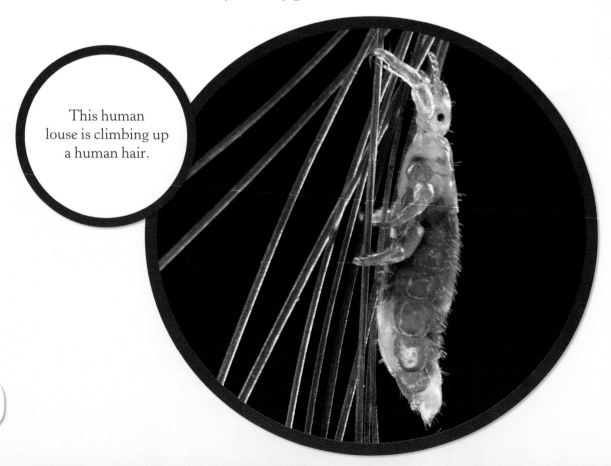

This human louse is climbing up a human hair.

A rabbit flea's body is covered in backward-pointing bristles and spikes that help it to stick to the host. A hungry flea looking for food can jump 600 times every hour.

Fleas

Fleas live in a similar way to lice, but they look very different. Lice are flattened from top to bottom, but fleas are flattened sideways. This makes it easy for them to move around through fur or feathers. All fleas have piercing and sucking mouthparts. Some fleas live on their hosts, but others live in the animal's nest or burrow. They jump onto their host when they want to feed.

Fleas lay rounded, smooth eggs that fall to the ground. When the eggs hatch, blind, wriggling **larvae** emerge and feed on the dried droppings of the adult fleas. Once fully grown, each larva spins a **cocoon** and becomes a **pupa**. The adult flea can stay inside the cocoon for up to 20 weeks, waiting for a host animal to come by.

The biggest difference between fleas and lice is the way they move around. Lice walk, but fleas can jump 20 times their own height. They use this jumping power to get on and off host animals.

The number of different types of living **organisms** in the world is often called **biodiversity**. Sadly, all over the world, **species** of living organisms are becoming **extinct**. This means that these organisms no longer exist on Earth. There are many different reasons for this. Extinction has always happened—some species die out and other species evolve (change). But today people are changing the world in ways that affect all other species.

People are damaging rivers, lakes, oceans, and seas. We are polluting the air and the water. We have overfished the oceans, driving many species to the verge of extinction. Our use of fossil fuels, such as oil and gas, is causing global warming. Global warming is a rise in Earth's average temperature and a change in weather patterns. When the temperature and the weather change, it can have a serious effect on living things, including insects.

Trouble in the tropics?

Scientists fear that insects in the tropics will be more affected by the temperature rises of global warming than insects in cooler areas. They think that insects like this butterfly are already living at the limit of their temperature tolerance, and they have relatively few ways of keeping themselves cool. If global temperatures continue to rise, they will die out. On the other hand, insect populations in traditionally cold areas could explode!

Insects play an essential role in **pollinating** many of the plants we use as food. Insect extinctions could cause terrible problems for humans, too.

If insects change their habitats as the planet warms up, we may find malaria mosquitoes spreading disease beyond the warm climates they live in now. Already, the cattle disease bluetongue is a problem in the southern United States. This is carried by midges, which are living longer and overwintering, increasing the spread of disease.

This mosquito is half-full of human blood. Female mosquitos can pass on the disease malaria.

What can be done?

To help prevent more insects from becoming extinct, people need to take care of Earth, protecting the places where insects live. If global warming can be stopped, many species will be saved. Biodiversity is important—we need as many species of insects as possible for the future.

Glossary

abdomen lower part of an insect's body

adapt gradually change to fit into a habitat

arthropod animal with an outer skeleton and jointed limbs

biodiversity different types of organisms around the world

camouflage when the shape and coloring of an insect make it difficult to spot

cell smallest unit of life

class in classification, large grouping of living things

cocoon covering of silk spun by some insect larvae when they become pupae

complete metamorphosis life cycle where insects begin life as larvae, then become pupae, and finally adults

compound eyes eyes made up of many small, simple eyes working together

digest break down food in the body

digestive system part of an animal's body that breaks down food so that it can be absorbed into the body

extinct when a species has died out and no longer exists

family in classification, a family is a grouping of living things that is larger than a genus but smaller than an order

fossil remains of an ancient living creature found in rocks

gene structure by which all living things pass on characteristics to the next generation

genus (plural **genera**) in classification, a grouping of living things that is larger than a species but smaller than a family

host animal or plant that another animal lives on

incomplete metamorphosis life cycle where the young change from looking similar to adults, to becoming adults, by growing wings and molting

kingdom in classification, the largest grouping of living things (for example, animals)

larvae (singular **larva**) the young of insects

mate (a) verb, to create young; (b) noun, an animal's partner

metamorphosis change

microorganism tiny living thing that can only be seen through a microscope

molt for insects, shedding the outer skin

nectar sweet liquid produced by some flowers

nymph young stage of an insect that undergoes incomplete metamorphosis

order in classification, an order is a group larger than a family but smaller than a class

organism living thing

parasite living thing that lives and feeds on or inside another living thing (its host)

phylum (plural **phyla**) in classification, a phylum is a group larger than a class but smaller than a kingdom

pollen yellow powder produced by flowers

pollinate transfer of pollen from male to female flower parts

predator animal that hunts other animals

prey animal that is hunted for food

pupa (plural **pupae**) hard, protective case in which an insect larva turns into an adult

segment part of an animal's body

species group of living things that are all similar and can reproduce together

30

Books

Eyewitness: Insect. New York: Dorling Kindersley, 2008.

Greenaway, Theresa. *DK Big Book of Bugs.* New York: Dorling Kindersley, 2000.

McEvey, Shane F. *Bugs.* Philadelphia: Chelsea House, 2001.

Pyers, Greg. *Classifying Animals: Why Am I an Insect?* Chicago: Raintree, 2006.

Snedden, Robert. *Living Things: Insects.* Mankato, Minn.: Smart Apple Media, 2009.

Websites

http://kids.yahoo.com/animals/insects
On this web page there are lots of links to information about individual insects.

www.ent.iastate.edu/imagegallery/
You can see images of many different insects on this web page.

www.si.edu/Encyclopedia_SI/nmnh/buginfo/start.htm
You will find lots of links to more information about insects on this web page.

www.mnh.si.edu
This is the website of the National Museum of Natural History in Washington, D.C.

www.historyforkids.org/scienceforkids/biology/animals/arthropods
Find out more about arthropods on this web page.